# Native American Women

## Three Who Changed History

*Gloria Steger Linkey*

SEACOVE PUBLISHING

Gloria Linkey@aol.com

# Native American Women

## Three Who Changed History

Gloria Stiger Linkey

Illustrations by Sally Steidel

Published by
Seacove Publishers
Seaside, Oregon 97138

ISBN 978-0-615-47239-3

Printed in the United States of America

This book is dedicated
to my two wonderful daughters
Victoria and Darci
and to the lovely woman
who calls me "Mumsie"
Margaret Ann

To my sister
Patricia

And in memory of my parents
who raised me with much
love and devotion
Ray and Lydia Stiger

# CONTENTS

# ACKNOWLEDGEMENTS

I **HAVE BEEN BLESSED** with three of the most wonderful friends, Meriel Cline, Mary Cornell and Lou Ann Baty Smith. They have listened to me talk about this book for over a year and never once complained. To have friends like these, I am indeed fortunate.

Jan Bono who has been my editor and mentor throughout the writing. Sally Steidel, did the realistic and beautiful drawings. JoAnne Danton who supplied the photographs and Sally Freeman checked my information on Lewis and Clark and kept me on tract with my quotes. Tom Wilson, who is one of the leading experts on the Lewis and Clark journey, has also been of tremendous assistance to me. Angel Sobotta, the lovely Nez Perce woman whom I the privilege of meeting, who spoke so lovingly about Watkuese and inspired me to continue my search for the truth about these Native American Women.

I'd also like to thank the Pacific Northwest Living Historians, a group of dedicated men and women who are instrumental in presenting and preserving authentic Northwest history, and who graciously allowed me to become a member of the organization. Without their support, and dedication, none of this could have been accomplished.

To my many other friends who are so passionate about history, The Lewis and Clark Trail Heritage Foundation, both locally and nationally, and all of the wonderful people I have met while giving speeches about these three women, thank you. Without the help that each of you have given me, this book could not have been written.

To one of the most knowledgeable and dedicated person I know about the Lewis & Clark journey, Roger Wendlick, I cannot thank you enough.

# PROLOGUE

SACAGAWEA is pronounced Sa-cog-a-we-a. Watkuese is pronounced Walk-coo-wees. Dorion, using the French pronunciation is DeRion. However the English pronunciation would be Dor-e-on.

Sacagawea is the thread that ties all three women together. She had the opportunity to meet Watkuese on the journey west with Lewis and Clark. She could have met Marie Dorion when Marie was traveling with the Astor Party on the way to the Pacific Coast.

Every attempt has been made on my part to be as accurate to the facts as possible. There are many untold parts of the Watkuese story, but in order to tell this remarkable tale in the oral tradition of the Nez Perce, it is important not to embellish any part of the story. I wish I could tell readers where Watkuese ended up in Canada, how many years she was held captive, how many years she lived with her husband, and most importantly, how many miles she walked to arrive back at her homeland. All we know for sure is that is was "many season" or "many moons."

The journals of Lewis and are written very factually, so there is little emotion in them. No one knows what thoughts went through the mind of Sacagawea when she saw the Pacific Ocean, so that part is left to our imagination.

I could find no historical record determining the sex of Marie's child born on the trail. Also there is no accurate information regarding the meeting between Marie and Sacagawea, when they were both traveling the Missouri River.

The important parts of the stories are what these remarkable women accomplished. They were brave, courageous women, and are definitely role models for the young people of today.

# CHAPTER 1

# SACAGAWEA: THE EARLY YEARS TO FORT MANDAN

SACAGAWEA, the Shoshoni woman who traversed the country with Lewis and Clark, faced many traumatic events before she was even 10 years old. She had been kidnapped by the Hidatsas, separated from her Shoshoni family, and taken far away from her own people to another part of the country where the language and customs were not familiar to her.

At the time of the kidnapping, Sacagawea thought she saw her dear brother, Cameahwait, killed in the raid. Although all these events had a profound affect on her, she was good-natured and calm, never bitter or vengeful.

Sacagawea was born a Lemhi Shoshoni in the part of the country that is near the Idaho/Montana border. After she was kidnapped, she was raised by a Hidatsa family in the region of North Dakota.

Fortunately for her, the Hidatsas did not have slaves. After her capture, Sacagawea was given to a family to replace a child who had died. Throughout her time with them, she was treated as any other family member. It is possible that both her biological mother and father were killed in the raid, and perhaps that is why no one from her tribe came looking for her.

In many ways, Sacagawea had an easier life with the Hidatsas than she would have had with the Shoshoni Nation. With the Hidatsas, there was no fear of raids from neighboring tribes because they lived next to the Mandans, and the Mandans provided them protection. The Mandans numbered around 4,500 people at that time. The tribes shared what they had with each other, and when hunting buffalos, they combined their forces, making the hunt naturally more successful. This was of great benefit to both tribes.

Sacagawea adapted quite well to her new way of life. Her calm disposition was of great value to her. By embracing the best of the two cultures, Shoshoni and Hidatsa, she became an extremely confident young lady. She had many innate talents and she developed several useful skills. Among these was finding food, making clothes, and dressing and processing animals skins. She assisted in preparing for winter and taking care of her adopted family. All of these traits would be of great advantage to her in her life ahead.

Sacagawea was married to Toussaint Charbonneau when she was just 14 or 15 years old. Charbonneau was more than twice her age, approximately 36 years old. One version of their story is that he won her in a game of chance, but this may not be completely accurate. It is more likely that she was given in marriage by her Hidatsa parents.

Although Charbonneau was already married to Otter Woman, another young Shoshoni girl, it was customary to take a second wife. Being the wife of a trader-trapper was a position of great respect. Sacagawea's adopted family would have looked favorably upon this marriage and received a generous dowry from Charbonneau.

The traditional European-American custom expects the bride's family to present a dowry to the husband. In the Native American culture, the potential husband must show his gratitude to the family of his future wife.

The historic customs and traditions of the Native Americans may seem strange to us today, but it is very important we not judge these people by our standards. Each tribe had its own rules and regulations for an orderly existence. These rules were sometimes complex and difficult for Americans to understand and it is this misunderstanding that prompted more than a few disputes between the two cultures.

Sacagawea lived as well as could be expected as the second wife of Charbonneau. There is nothing written to suggest any kind of master/slave relationship existed between them. She was pregnant with their first child when Lewis and Clark and the U. S. Army expedition arrived at the Mandan Village in October, 1804. The expedition had been traveling up the Missouri River in three boats, including a keel boat, and two pirogues. A pirogue is a long, narrow boat with a sail.

The Mandans welcomed the expedition and proved to be quite helpful to them. They shared food with the men of the expedition and allowed them to stay safely in a part of the country where they might not have otherwise been safe.

This was considered an agriculture nation, as the Mandans raised quite a few vegetables for food and trading. Corn, squash, beans and sunflowers were four of their main products.

There were good hunters with the expedition. They had guns, and with horses borrowed from the Mandans, proved very valuable in securing meat for the winter months ahead.

Along the banks of the Missouri River were groves of cottonwood trees, and the soldiers quickly chopped some down to build their winter quarters. Construction began on November 3, 1804, according to Private Joseph Whitehouse, one of the expedition soldiers.

These quarters were located on the north bank of the Missouri River, directly opposite the lower Mandan village. It was a well- built structure, with two rows of cabins, a parade ground in the middle, a gate, and a sentry post. The swivel gun, a small cannon from one of the boats, was mounted on the outer wall of the fort. The walls were at least 18 feet high. This was done in case there would be an attack by anyone, either the Native Americans, or the British. They called their quarters Fort Mandan.

From the beginning of construction, the Mandans and Hidatsa frequently came across the river to view the work in progress. Friendly trading often took place between the two races.

Although the weather was brutally cold, the men of the expedition hunted often, bringing in buffalo. The buffalo skins were used for protection against the cold weather, and made ideal robes and blankets.

The expedition shared their knowledge of medicine with the Mandans and treated quite a variety of their ailments, including frostbite. The methods of handling frostbite were warming the frostbitten parts slowly, and if that did not work, then amputation of the affected party of the body was necessary.

Captain Lewis was forced to amputate the toes of both feet of a young Mandan Indian. This young man and his father had gone hunting and only had a buffalo robe to keep them warm at night. The young man's feet had become uncovered during the night, and he had received severe frostbite on his feet. Captain Clark recorded the temperature the following morning being -40 degrees F. On the February 23, Captain Clark reported in his journal that the young man had recovered quite nicely and his father took him home.

The Captains also doctored a few cases of abscess on the young children. Their knowledge of medicine, though limited by some standards, was indeed welcomed by the Mandans.

The most common medical problem was syphilis, not only among the Native Americans, but also among the men on the expedition. The standard treatment consisted of using mercury as a curative.

Perhaps Captain Lewis' most challenging medical task was during the birth of Sacagawea's child. Sacagawea was a young girl, and quite small, thus making the birth of her first child extremely difficult.

On February 11, 1805, she gave birth to a fine baby boy, and the circumstances of the birth are recorded in the Journals of Lewis & Clark: "about five o'clock this evening one of the wives of Charbono was delivered of a fine boy. It is worthy of remark that this was the first child which this woman had boarn and as in common in such case her labour was tedious and the pain violet. Mr. Jessome informed me that he had frequently administered a small portion of the rattle of the rattle snake, which he assured me had never failed to produce the desired effect, that of hastening the birth of the child: having the rattle of a snake by me I gave it to him and he administered two rings of it to the woman broken in small pieces with the fingers and added to a small quantity of water. Whether this medicine was truly the cause or not I shall not undertake to determine, but I was informed that she had not taken it more than ten minutes before she brought forth perhaps this remedy may be worthy of future experiments, but I must confess that I want faith as to its efficacy."[1]

Fortunately for modern society, and rattlesnakes, this method of childbirth never caught on with the medical practitioners of today. There are many more proven options in hastening the birth of a child. It is very interesting however, to have this credible reference of child birthing among the Native Americans.

Among the expedition were blacksmiths. These men were quite popular with the Mandans, as they were very proficient at repairing axes. In addition, and perhaps even more valuable, the blacksmiths were capable of repairing hoes, and other instruments that were vital to the agricultural success of the Mandans.

After all the mending of farm equipment has been completed, Private John Shields, a skilled blacksmith, turned his attention to the manufacturing of battle axes. These were highly prized by the Mandans, and Shields was very efficient in producing them. This was done in exchange for corn and other vegetables.

Charbonneau had presented himself to the Captains as being an excellent guide, trapper, and interpreter, and wished to

---

[1]  Gary E. Moulton, The Definitive Journals of Lewis & Clark, Lincoln, Nebraska: University of Nebraska, volume 3, page 291

accompany the expedition to the Pacific Coast. Charbonneau had been trapping, trading and hunting in this area for approximately six years and was very well acquainted with the land. While he was well-versed in the geography of the river system, he was, in fact, deathly afraid of the river and could not swim.

However, Charbonneau also informed the Captains right away that he would not stand guard duty and some of the other tasks that were assigned to the men of the expedition. After Charbonneau presented his list of what he would not do, the Captains made the decision not to hire him. A few days later, a very repentant Charbonneau presented himself to the Captains, and requested to be a part of the expedition, saying he would do whatever duties were deemed necessary during their journey.

Perhaps it was Sacagawea who contributed to Charbonneau changing his mind. Here was an opportunity for her to see the Shoshonis, her people, and she may have been looking forward to this journey. Sacagawea was a person of great poise and intelligence. She was not a hothead like her husband, and she could see the value in having her husband become a member of the expedition.

After the Captains and Charbonneau came to an agreement over his duties and pay, Charbonneau chose Sacagawea to accompany him on the trip. Jean Baptiste, their son, was just six weeks old when he started the journey with his mother and father. Sacagawea had recovered quite quickly from childbirth and was very proud of her son. It was the custom of the Native Americans for grandmothers and aunts to assist in raising a child and to teach them the traditions and customs. Sacagawea would not have this help with Jean Baptiste for the next two years.

We have no record as to what happened to Charbonneau's other wife, Otter Woman. Sacagawea's admirable qualities and skills, especially her ability to translate Shoshoni into Hidatsa, which Charbonneau could then translate into French for one of the French interpreters, may have been one of the deciding factors to have her accompany the men. Also, Sacagawea had a calm disposition, which would be very helpful on this long and difficult journey.

One of the most pressing problems would be communicating with the various tribes of the Native Americans. President Jefferson had requested as much information about the tribes as it was possible for the expedition to obtain. The gathering of the various sounds which constituted the native language was highly important to Captain Lewis, and he made every effort to record as much as he could of all the languages.

Another one of Sacagawea's skills was in food collection. She was especially good at collecting Jerusalem artichokes for the men. She found these by poking the earth with a sharp stick and then digging for them. She also found wild licorice and large quantities of the root called the white apple. These two vegetables became extremely important to the men to supplement their all-meat diet and also for the prevention of scurvy.

# CHAPTER 2

# FORT MANDAN
# TO THE SHOSHONIS

ON APRIL 7, 1805, Sacagawea set out on the journey of a lifetime, accompanying the Lewis & Clark Expedition to the Pacific Ocean and back again. She was the lone woman on the expedition of 31 men, and had a small baby to take care of.

What would happen to Jean Baptiste if she became ill on the journey? How would this small child survive if she was unable to provide milk for her son? How would she protect her child from the hazards of this trip? To a less confident and skilled woman, these concerns may have been a problem, however there is no record of Sacagawea pondering these questions. She apparently took it all in stride.

It is probable that York, Captain Clark's servant, was of some assistance to Sacagawea in caring for the baby. York, being born on Captain Clark's plantation, would have been accustomed to being around small children, and may have been able to help with Jean Baptiste. We do know that it was the duty of York and Sacagawea to erect the tent which served as sleeping quarters for the Captains, George Drouillard, and the Charbonneaus each evening, and to take it down in the morning.

In many history books, Sacagawea has been described as a guide. This is an incorrect description of her duties with the expedition. She was able to guide them for a small portion of the journey, only to the Shoshoni village where she had lived when she was kidnapped.

It is Sacagawea's other qualities that were more important. She was a hard worker, taking all of her assigned tasks and completing them well without a whimper of complaint. She was extremely confident and very calm in all situations. Sacagawea and her small son provided the men on the expedition with a glimpse of true family life they had left behind and would not see again for two years.

One of the most important tasks that faced Sacagawea, was making certain that Jean Baptiste slept through the night and that his crying did not disturb the men. After a long day of very hard work and travel, the men needed a good night's sleep to insure they would have the energy to do it all over again the following day. This could have been a difficult task, especially when Jean Baptiste was teething, but Sacagawea was certainly capable of handling the situation. Sacagawea's responsibilities were not too much for this young girl and it is admirable how she adeptly handled everything she was required to do.

We have an example of the composure that Sacagawea exhibited on May 14, 1805. Captain Clark writes, "we proceeded on verry well until about 6 oClock a squawl of wind Struck our Sale broad Side and turned the pirogue nearly over, and in this Situation the Perogue remained until the Sale was cut down in which time She nearly filed with water—the articles which floated out were nearly all caught by the Squar who was in the rear. This accident had like to have cost us deerly for in this pirogue were embarked our papers, Instruments, books, medicine, a great proportion of our merchandize, and in short, almost every article indispensibly necessary to further the views, or insure the success of the enterprise in which, we are now launched to the distance of 2,2-oomiles."[2]

---

[2]  Gary E.Moulton, *The Definitive Journals of Lewis & Clark*, Lincoln, Nebraska, University of Nebraska, Volume 4, page 154

The "squar" Clark refers to is Sacagawea, who not only tended to her son, but calmly rescued their supplies while the men attempted to manage the pirogue.

Captain Lewis records in his journal on May 16, 1805: "the morning was fair and the day proved favorable to our operations; by 4oClock in the evening our Instruments, Medicine, merchandize provision &c, were perfectly dryed, repacked and put on board the pirogue. The loss we sustained was not to great as we had at first apprehended, our medicine sustained the greatest injury, several articles of which were intirely spoiled, and many others considerably injured, the balance of our losses consisted of some gardin seeds, a small quantity of gunpowder, and a few culinary articles which fell overboard and sunk, the Indian woman to whom I ascribe equal fortitude and resolution, with any person on board at the time of the accident, caught and preserved most of the light articles which were washed overboard." [3]

Fortitude and resolution—high praise indeed from the Captains. Again, Sacagawea exhibited composure and calmness in the face of terrifying losses. Had the pirogue capsized, undoubtedly Sacagawea and her child most likely would have drowned, as there is no record of her being able to swim.

While she was rescuing all of the items so important to the expedition, it is recorded in the journals that Charbonneau began fervently praying to his God in French for safety. Only after Private Cruzatte threatened to shoot him if he did not take hold of the tiller, does Charbonneau comes to his senses and do everything in his power to right the pirogue and set it straight.

---

[3] Gary E. Moulton, *The Definitive Journals of Lewis & Clark*, Lincoln, Nebraska, University of Nebraska, volume 4, page 157

Sacagawea's importance to the expedition is again emphasized a little later on, when both Captains commented in their journals as to how ill she had become. Captain Lewis wrote on June 16, 1805: "found the Indian woman extremely ill and much reduced by her indisposition, this gave me some concern as well for the poor object herself, then with a young child in her arms, as from the consideration of her being our only dependence for a friendly negociation with the Snake Indians on whom we depend for horses to assist us in our portage from the Missouri to the Columbia River." [4] Snake Indian is another name for the Shoshoni Native American.

However, on June 19, 1805, Lewis once again wrote: "the Indian woman was much better this morning she walked out and gathered a considerable quantity of the white apples of which she eat so heartily in their raw state, together with a considerable quantity of dryed fish without my knowledge that she complained very much that her fever again returned. I rebuked Sharbono severely for suffering her to indulge herself with such food he being privy to it and having been previously told what she must only eat." [5]

Sacagawea fully recovered and, of course, continued to be of assistance to the expedition. This is but another example of her fortitude and perseverance. A mother's love for her child was extremely strong in Sacagawea and this devotion to her duty to

[4]  Gary E. Moulton, *The Definitive Journals of Lewis & Clark*, Lincoln, Nebraska, University of Nebraska, Volume 4, page 299
[5]  Gary E. Moulton, *The Definitive Journals of Lewis & Clark*, Lincoln, Nebraska, University of Nebraska, Volume 4, page 309

protect and care for Jean Baptiste was upmost in her thoughts.

Shortly after that, Sacagawea became quite excited. She recognized Beaver Head Rock. She told Captain Lewis that it was near the summer retreat of her nation beyond the mountains. Finally they were nearing the Shoshoni people.

Here Captain Lewis made a journal entry that is a little dismissive of Sacagawea. He states that she shows no emotion at being near her people again and in his opinion, "if she has enough to eat and a few trinkets she would be happy." [6]

Perhaps the reason she showed no emotion was because she was so well-settled into her new life that she did not even consider returning to the Shoshonis. If she believed her family had been killed in the raid when she was kidnapped, she might have been concerned about returning to the tribe where she would have no family to protect her.

Captain Lewis took a few men, including interpreter George Drouillard, and they proceeded on ahead to locate the Shoshoni village. For reasons unknown, Captain Lewis did not take Sacagawea with him and she remained with Captain Clark. Unfortunately, Captain Lewis had trouble communicating with the Shoshonis as he was not proficient in either their oral or sign language.

A Shoshoni brave on horseback was then spotted. However, when the Captain approached him, the man turned and rode off. He was concerned as to who these men were.

Captain Lewis then saw an elderly woman with two younger women. Once again, we see how important women were to the

---

[6] Gary E. Moulton, *The Definitive Journals of Lewis & Clark*, Lincoln, Nebraska, University of Nebraska, Volume 5, page 9

success of the expedition. While one of the younger women ran toward the rocks to hide, the elderly woman and a girl about 12 years old sat on the ground with heads bowed. This was a sign that they expected to be killed. Captain Lewis gently lifted the women to her feet and presented her with small trinkets. He instructed Drouillard to have her call the other woman out of hiding, so she would not run off and alert the men of the tribe.

Captain Lewis kept repeating "tab-ba-bone", which he thought meant "white person" in their language. Through sign language, Drouillard persuades the women to take them to their village.

After approximately two miles, 60 warriors suddenly appeared. They were dressed for war. They could have been warned by the Shoshoni on horseback whom Captain Lewis had spotted, and they were uncertain if these men were their enemy, the Blackfeet, or some other hostile tribe.

The elderly woman ran to the warriors and showed them all the trinkets that Captain Lewis had given her. The warriors understood that the men were friendly and welcomed them.

Without the assistance of this woman, we do not know if there would have been an outbreak of hostilities, but it was quite evident this woman played a very important role in keeping the peace and allowing the expedition to meet with the Shoshonis.

After Captain Clark and the rest of the expedition arrived at the Shoshoni Village, the first person Sacagawea recognized was a young woman who had been kidnapped at the same time as she had. The young woman had managed to escape from her captors and made her way back to her people. Their reunion was quite joyous. The two young women hugged and talked. Both seemed very glad to realize the other one was alive and well. Sacagawea showed off Jean Baptiste, who was healthy and quite well-fed. In comparison, Shoshoni children were very thin and appeared to be hungry.

The Shoshoni people had been forced to live in the mountains of Montana due to continuous pressure from their enemies. There was little food where they lived, not much more than berries and some roots. Meat was difficult to obtain, and hunger prevailed throughout the village.

Life was very hard for these people. They had difficulty hunting. Their enemies had many guns, and the Shoshoni had few. Their horses gave them some advantage in hunting, but without guns they were at the mercy of their well-armed enemies.

According to the journals, they were happy people and quite helpful. The Shoshonis provided crudely drawn maps for the expedition and valuable information about crossing the mountains. When one of the hunters, George Drouillard, shot a deer, Captain Lewis gave half to the people of the village, and they were very grateful.

The customs of the Shoshoni were quite different from those of the Mandan or Hidatsa. For example, the men of the family had complete authority over the women and when a girl was born, the father immediately pledged her in marriage to a suitable male. The girl lived with her parents until she reached puberty, then was given in marriage to her husband. It was common for the men to take two or three wives, therefore there were more women and children in the village than men.

While at the Shoshoni village, the man who had been pledged to become Sacagawea's husband was living there. Although according to Shoshoni culture he could have claimed Sacagawea as his wife, he declined, as she had had a child by another man.

Originally, President Jefferson had requested that the men find the Northwest Passage, a presumed waterway, so the United States could establish a trade route to the west and on to Asia. The Captains now knew there was not a river passage to the west and they would have to travel by horseback to cross the mountains. Obtaining horses was crucial to the expedition. The Shoshoni had large herds of horses that were fast and in good condition.

After the Captains spent an evening smoking the peace pipe with Chief Cameahwait, the next morning they requested a council with the Chief. Sacagawea attended this important council meeting, along with Charbonneau, and Private LaBiche.

In order to relay a message, it had to be translated into four languages; Cameahwait spoke in Shoshoni to Sacagawea, who then translated to Charbonneau in Hidatsa, who in turn translated to Private Labiche in French, who translated in English to the Captains Lewis and Clark.

At the council, Sacagawea, being a proper woman, had her eyes downcast and would not have spoken unless it was necessary to the translation. Suddenly, she looked closely at the Chief, and crying and laughing at the same time, she managed to reveal that Cameahwait was her own dear brother, the one she thought she had seen killed in the raid when she was kidnapped.

During the rest of the council, she contained herself and completed her duties as requested by the Captains. Sacagawea's heart must have been bursting with joy and pride at the thought of her brother becoming Chief.

To become a Chief of the Shoshoni tribe was not a matter of lineage or heredity. This honor was given to an individual who had proven his bravery, intelligence, and capability of leading his people. What a wonderful tribute the Shoshonis paid to her brother. Sacagawea always believed her brother possessed all the qualities to be a chief, and for the tribe to honor him this way proved Sacagawea's pride in her brother was well-founded.

Cameahwait did not tell Sacagawea at that time that both her mother and father were dead. She learned that later. She also heard she had a nephew by another brother who was away at the time, but this was all that was left of her immediate family.

All Sacagawea had to say to her brother was to let them have the horses, only if they let me stay with my people. No one would have understood this request in Shoshoni. With her brother being Chief, Sacagawea would have had protection and a place of respect in the village. But she did not ask to stay.

Though the journey would prove to be long and difficult, Sacagawea would see it through. Now she had a better sense of her duty to the expedition. She would do nothing that would diminish her in the eyes of her brother, and with fierce determination and pride, she continued on this incredible journey.

When the translations were completed, the expedition secured all the horses they needed. Sacagawea then had an opportunity to have a reunion with her brother and they shared happy remembrances of the days of their youth. She was very proud to show off her son, Jean Baptiste, to his uncle.

Jean Baptiste was quite a hit with the entire village. Sacagawea had taken very good care of him and he was a plump, happy child. This was in contrast to some of the young children in the village and may have been one of the compelling reasons Sacagawea decided not to stay with the Shoshonis. She and Jean Baptiste were much better off continuing with the expedition and they certainly had a better life with the Hidatsa than they would have had if she stayed with the Shoshonis. Even though her brother held a very important position in the village, he was helpless in securing enough food for the people under his care.

While the expedition was with the Shoshoni Nation, it is well documented that Charbonneau struck Sacagawea. Captain Clark quickly reprimanded Charbonneau for this foolish act. It is not fully understood if Charbonneau committed this act to show his power over Sacagawea, to impress the Captains, or simply out of anger.

Apparently the Captains thought this showed great disrespect for the Shoshonis, and Charbonneau was instructed not to hit his wife again.

What effect did this act of cowardliness on Charbonneau's part have on Sacagawea? Was it enough for her to consider changing her mind and seek asylum with her people? Would she risk Jean Baptist's health and general welfare to rid herself of her husband? Charbonneau was not a perfect man, and was known to have struck both Sacagawea and Otter Woman on several previous occasions.

Sacagawea's sense of love, duty and integrity were stronger than her desire to leave her husband, and within a few seconds, she made the decision to stay with the expedition and her husband. Perhaps it was due to the Captains' forcible demand that Charbonneau behave himself; he never struck Sacagawea again on the trip.

Chief Cameahwait had already provided the Captains with a roughly drawn map of the area that lay ahead of them and they secured the services of a guide, Old Toby. Sacagawea was the translator between Old Toby and the Captains.

Cameahwait informed the Captains that the passage through the mountains was dangerous and difficult, with very little game to hunt. The Captains felt that if the Shoshoni could pass through this area with women and children, so could the expedition.

Sacagawea proved her worth again in assisting the expedition in finding roots and berries for survival, as the trip proved to be as arduous as Chief Cameahwait had predicted.

All they had to eat during this time was the portable soup with a few berries, and some roots added. One of the hunters managed to shoot a grouse and this was about all the meat they could find. Not much protein for the 31 men of the expedition. Without Sacagawea's ability to find a few edible roots and berries, it could have been disastrous.

By the time they had reached the Nez Perce Nation, they were near starvation. Several of the men were quite ill from lack of nourishment. Fortunately, the Nez Perce helped them get back on their feet.

Sacagawea could relax for a bit and regain her health. Now she was in the company of other women. She had proved her abilities and worth as part of the expedition. She had rescued valuable supplies from the pirogue, found roots and berries to help prevent scurvy in the men, was instrumental in the efforts of securing horses from the Shoshonis, and completed all of her assigned tasks without complaint.

However, the journey was not over. What other experiences awaited this brave young lady as she continued on with the Captains and the men of the expedition?

# CHAPTER 3

# WATKUESE

**ARRIVING AT THE NEZ PERCE NATION** on September 21, 1805, Captain Clark made a brief entry in his journal, speaking of a particular woman of the tribe: "one had formerly been taken by the Minitarries of the north & Seen white, men"[7]

Neither the Captains nor any of the men in the expedition knew the extreme importance of this woman and how she would change the history of their journey with four simple words which effected their very survival.

Watkuese was a Nez Perce woman, apparently in her late twenties, when the journal entry was written. Her story is told in the oral history of the Nez Perce, and every attempt has been made to be as accurate as possible in telling her remarkable tale.

As a young girl, either 10 or 12 years old, her Nez Perce family had gone hunting to the buffalo country with others from her tribe. They resided among the friendly Salish people.

---

[7] Gary E.Moulton, *The Definitive Journals of Lewis & Clark*, Lincoln, Nebraska, University of Nebraska, Volume 5, page 226

Here, life was good for them, as there was excellent hunting, which provided ample food for all. The Nez Perce family had procured a good supply of hides and dried meat, and were ready to return to their own tribe, when a party of Minitarries swept down upon them.

The Minitarries were stronger than the Nez Perce, and had many guns. They killed many people and took all their meat. Watkuese was kidnapped and carried away from her family and homeland. It is not known if any other women were carried off during this raid.

Watkuese's experience was similar to that of Sacagawea, except Watkuese was not treated kindly by her captors. She was physically and sexually abused by the men and forced to do hard labor by the women of the tribe.

Her regular duties often included gathering fuel for the fires. Chopping and hauling wood was exhaustive work. Scraping the flesh off the heavy hides and hanging them to dry also taxed her physical strength. She was treated as a slave, and did anything that the other women did not wish to do.

Watkuese traveled through many tribes of Native Americans as her original captors migrated east. She was sold to other tribes along the way, and it is generally conceded she ended up in eastern Canada. There is no definite area stated where her eastward journey ended.

After suffering for years at the hands of her captives, she was either sold or traded to a white man living in that region. The only measurement of time we have is that many seasons, or many moons, passed, before this event occurred. Here she resided with other white people, and learned some of their ways.

She had a baby boy and apparently lived a good life among the white people. Her husband was kind to her, perhaps displaying the first compassion she had known since being kidnapped. There is no definite number of years she resided as a wife to this white man.

Watkuese desired to return to her home and live among her own people. One of her neighbors had informed her that her husband would soon leave for his native country across the ocean, either England or France, and intended to take his family with him. This meant Watkuese would never see her people again and would be living in a foreign land.

By this time, her son was able to sit up and crawl. With the help of her white neighbors, who gave her some food, a knife, and a hatchet, she left her husband, took the baby, and started her journey across the country. Her intention was to return to her people, the Nez Perce.

Armed with a knife and hatchet, food, courage and endurance, Watkuese started walking westward, following the sun. It is estimated she could have traveled well over 600 miles. She walked the entire way, carrying her baby on her back. Regardless of the weather, she continued on her journey, across plains, deserts and rivers.

It is difficult to tell how many months it took Watkuese to walk across the country. What dangers she faced are not fully recorded. Her only companions were the birds and friendly animals she spotted along the way. At times, she proceeded on her journey with absolute silence surrounding her. Her thoughts must have turned many times to her homeland and her people and this would have been what kept her going on this journey.

In the words of oral tradition, she states that the spirit of the Great Wolf went ahead of her. When she was tired and felt she could not go on, her spirit helper, the Wolf, was always there, showing her the way to go and encouraging her to continue. When danger was close by, the spirit caused a fog to appear and hid her from the enemies. This was her only protection. She expressed gratitude for this helpful act and always thanked her guardian spirit.

There were many dangers. She could slip and fall, be attacked by wolves, be swept away by the river, or be kidnapped again and taken to another tribe. Her enemies were everywhere. Persistence and moral strength were her constant companions as she traveled. Did she ever think that perhaps she had been foolish to leave her husband and home? There is nothing in her story to suggest that. Watkuese's desire to return to her people was the strongest and most compelling reason for continuing this journey.

Once when she was faced with the task of crossing a large river, she cut branches from a tree to construct a raft. Before she completed the crossing, a bear loomed out of the river just before she reached the opposite shore. With one blow of her hatchet, she killed the bear, and hurried on.

Unfortunately, Watkuese left her hatchet on the raft, and miles later when she discovered it missing, she did not go back to retrieve this valuable tool.

After months of travel, what little food she had when she left her husband or had been able to secure along the way, was gone. She had no milk for her baby to nurse and the baby grew weaker by the day.

Finally Watkuese came upon an abandoned hunting camp.

There she found a bone with some dried meat and built a small fire to cook the meat. Perhaps it was too late to save the baby, or maybe the meat was spoiled. The baby died shortly after she tried to feed him. She dug a small grave, then covered it with rocks so animals would not find it.

Now she was truly alone, except for her spirit guide. Weeping and stumbling, Watkuese walked on toward her homeland. She had no idea how far she had traveled, or how far she had to go to get home to her people. Always the thought of her people and homeland encouraged her to continue on.

She came to the last mountains separating her from her homeland. She knew she did not have the strength to cross these high mountain peaks. She lay down and asked the Great Spirit to take her so she could join her baby in the spirit world. But her efforts to get this far would not be in vain.

# CHAPTER 4

# WATKUESE HOME COMING

A GROUP OF SALISH HUNTERS returning from a very successful hunting trip, found Watkuese, and gently placed her on a horse. They knew she belonged to the village of Red Bear, and that is where they took her. When the people of the village saw the hunters, they were astonished. At first they thought the men had stolen this woman from another tribe. But why would they take such a sickly woman?

As the men approached the village, the people recognized her as the daughter of a family that had left their tribe many moons ago to go hunting. She was Nez Perce, and they gave her the name Watkuese, which translated is, "Gone from home then come back."

Gently the women lifted her from the horse and carried her into one of the tents. There they made her a bed to lie upon, provided her with food, and slowly restored her to good health.

When Watkuese was stronger, she told them her story. First

the people did not believe her. How could a woman walk all that way with a small child? How had she survived?

The Nez Perce had never heard of pale-skinned people. Watkuese told of the many things the white people had and how their numbers were as many as the leaves on the trees. She called the white people So-yap-pos. Watkuese told of their homes, towns, and clothes. She told the Nez Perce people that someday the So-yap-pos would come to their village.

Watkuese told many tales of these strange people who lived far away across the country. People with upside down faces, which is how she described men with beards, and of other people who had different color eyes, hair and skin. She told them how one family of So-yap-pos had been kind and helped her escape. She spoke highly of the So-yap-pos, and remembered them with great fondness.

Watkuese repeated her story many times, so the people could remember it repeat it word for word. This is the way all the Nez Perce stories live on. Watkuese grew in stature and respect in the village. She gradually regained her health.

Watkuese was helpful to all the people, but she selected only easy chores to do, such as tending the fires and keeping track of the children, as she could no longer do heavy labor. As she tended the young children, did her thoughts return to her own small son? Did she wonder what he would have been like as a young man? Perhaps she pictured him as a tall, brave, and intelligent man, always ready to help wherever needed.

Perhaps her son would have been a great hunter, providing ample food for all the people. These were the thoughts that Watkuese lived with, but she shared them with no one else. She had loved her son and tried in all ways to protect him and keep him safe while on their journey. She had shed so many tears for the death of her son, she often felt she had no more tears left in her.

The seasons passed and Watkuese grew frail and weak. The effects of her arduous journey had taken its toll. Although she was probably not more than in her late twenties, she was now called Old Watkuese. Her face was lined with wrinkles of wisdom and strength. Regardless of her age, she was still a much-valued member of her village. The Nez Perce had great respect for the older generation and treated them very kindly.

One day some young boys came running into the village. They were very excited and told the people they had seen white men: So-yap-pos. One had hair the color of fire; one was all black. The most unusual condition was that they had a Shoshoni woman and her baby with them.

The presence of the woman and baby indicated these strangers were not a war party. A war party never traveled with a woman and child. Might these be the So-yap-pos that had helped Watkuese escape and return to her homeland? Could one of them be her husband? Would he have traveled this far to reclaim Watkuese as his wife? There was much talk in the village about this strange event.

The men of the expedition were tired and sick. They had not eaten for some time and were desperate for food. The people of the village provided food for these men. Most of the men ate greedily, became quite ill, and were unable to move for two or three days.

While the men lay down, Sacagawea had heard Captain Clark speak of the woman who had lived with white people. Sacagawea went in search of this woman and met Watkuese. What they specifically talked about is not known, but Sacagawea undoubtedly expressed sympathy for the loss of Watkuese's baby. Watkuese could have told of her experiences living with a white man, and her amazing journey across the country.

How it must have cheered Sacagawea to hear of another woman's adventure. Although their time together was short, it was a powerful experience for both women. Sacagawea realized that in spite of all her hardships, how fortunate she was to have the protection of Captain Clark and the men of the expedition.

The Nez Perce were a powerful nation. Everyone who went west or returned to the east had to pass through their land. They controlled central Idaho, and the eastern parts of Washington and Oregon.

The Nez Perce considered the expedition invaders of their land. They were quite alarmed at the sight Captain Clark's servant, a large black man named York, and thought he must be a warrior. This gave them concern as they did not know what the So-pay-pos had in mind. Would they prove to be enemies? The Nez Perce were more in number, but the So-pay-pos had guns and bullets. Some of the Nez Perce thought that York had magic powers and was of great strength.

The Nez Perce had another name for the expedition: Pai-yo-it. Translated it means "something that smells." The men of the expedition had not bathed for quite some time and their clothes were old and dirty. Having traveled all that way without a bath or the ability to wash their clothes, one can only image the offensive stench.

At first, the Nez Perce were content to leave the men alone. But after a few days, they realized the Sa-pay-pos' guns and many other possessions could be of great value to them. The Nez Perce had few guns, but their enemies, the Blackfeet, had many guns. The Blackfeet were supplied guns by the British on the Canadian border. Any tribe that could secure the great treasures of the So-yap-pos would be a strong nation and one to be feared among other nations.

At this point, the Nez Perce held a council with all their Chiefs and made the decision to kill these So-yap-pos and take their goods. Watkuese, close to passing on, heard this conversation. She asked the women who were with her in the tent to open the flap, so she could speak to the men.

The words she uttered to the council changed the history of our country. Her words were, "These men are So-yap-pos! Good men! Men like these were good to me. Do not kill them! Do them no harm!" [8]

Because of this very brave and courageous woman, and the respect the Nez Perce had for Watkuese, they decided to heed her words. As a result, Lewis and Clark and the men of the expedition were left alone to recuperate in safety.

After Watkuese spoke these words, she lay back down, and soon her spirit left her and she joined her child in the spirit world.

None of the men of the expedition knew of this remarkable woman or the words she spoke that saved their lives. It was only through the Nez Perce's oral history that this story, like the Corps of Discovery, survived.

After the expedition regained their health, the Nez Perce showed them a better and easier way to build their canoes. They were taught to burn the logs and then chop out the soft charred

---

[8]   Zoa L. Swayne, *Do Them No Harm!* Caldwell, Idaho, Caxton Press, page 42

wood, instead of digging out the green wood with axes. With five canoes made, the men of the expedition were ready to continue their journey to the Pacific Ocean. They branded their mounts and left them with the Nez Perce for safe keeping. On the journey back, they would reclaim their horses.

For the rest of the journey, the expedition traveled the waterways in canoes. The Nez Perce supplied the men with guides down the Clearwater River and on down the Snake River. Without the help of the Nez Perce Nation, the men might not have been able to continue their journey with such ease.

History owes quite a large debt of gratitude to these people and to Watkuese in particular. She deserves a place of honor when telling the story of the Lewis and Clark Expedition and especially in our history books.

Watkuese is responsible for the friendship that developed between the expedition and the Nez Perce people. For all her bravery, for speaking up and saving the expedition, she is only given a short sentence or two in the journals. Watkuese had great love for the Nez Perce people and her homeland. She traveled many miles to return to her people and endured severe hardships along the way. Her love and courage shines through her story, and these attributes are the qualities that made her such a remarkable woman.

# CHAPTER 5

# TO FORT CLATSOP

SACAGAWEA and the Corps of Discovery continued their journey. By now the men had regained their strength and soon reached the Columbia River. From the intersection of the Snake and Columbia Rivers on October 18, 1805, they could see Mt. Hood.

The Columbia was a magnificent river with rolling swells. The men felt they were very close to the end of their trip. At first, some of the men were confused by the roughness of the river and thought they had reached the ocean.

How pleased Sacagawea must have been to learn that the end of the journey was near. There would be rest and a shelter built to protect her and Jean Baptiste from the wet and cold weather as winter approached. But a storm arose, with high winds and continuous rain, and the men were unable to travel in their canoes. They were stranded on the rocks on the north side of the lower portion of the Columbia for several days and nights. The waves crashed the canoes against the rocks, threatening to break them apart.

The men were unable to dry their clothes, or get warm. They were pounded by driving rain and high winds. Both Captains said it was the most dismal place they had ever seen. This spot is called Dismal Nitch today, and is located along the banks of the Columbia River on the Washington side, four miles from the mouth of the river.

In the midst of this storm, imagine the men's surprise to see a group of Clatsop Native Americans crossing the great river in their canoes. The men marveled at their skill in navigating the

*Fort Clatsop, near Astoria. Photograph courtesy of Jo Ann Daton.*

*Site of original Salt Works, located in Seaside, Oregon. Photograph courtesy of Jo Ann Daton.*

*Dug Out Canoe at Fort Clatsop, Astoria, Oregon.*
*Photograph courtesy of Darci Bodin.*

*Dug Out Canoe, located at Netuel Landing, Fort Clatsop, Astoria, Oregon. Photograph courtesy of Jo Ann Daton.*

*Tillamook Head, located at Seaside, Oregon. Photograph courtesy of Jo Ann Daton.*

water. Their canoes were built much differently from the dugouts the expedition used. They were more aerodynamic, and easier to maneuver. Both Captains commented in their journals that these were the best canoe navigators they had ever seen.

Days later the storm subsided and the men were able to continue on around Point Ellice. They reached the site now called Station Camp.

Station Camp was a Chinook trading village. Much to the surprise of the men, they found many Chinooks wearing sailor clothes. They also saw large cooking pots, evidence that these people had traded with many ships at the mouth of the Columbia River. The Chinook women were very involved in the trading and this gave them stature and respect in the village. Sacagawea took note of everything she saw and heard.

The Chinooks were different from the other tribes they had seen. They were quite wealthy by native standards, due to all the trading they did with the ships that arrived from other countries. The Chinook Tribe controlled all the trading on the Columbia River, and in order to communicate with tribes farther up the river, they had developed the Chinookan jargon.

Jargon was a simplification of the original Chinook language with words from other languages mixed in to make it more understandable for all the various tribes living along the Columbia River. To this day, some Chinookan is still spoken among the tribes.

The most popular trade items were sea otter pelts. These pelts were taken to China, exchanged for tea, spices and beautiful China pottery, then taken back to the east coast of American and to Europe. This was a very profitable business for the ship owners of many countries, including England, Spain and Russia.

Beaver pelts were also very popular trade items. These pelts made very fine hats which were cutting-edge fashion and highly sought after on the east coast of America. It took three or four pelts to make one hat, and they were in constant demand. Traders and trappers could make their fortunes collecting these pelts.

The expedition had yet to see the Pacific Ocean. On November 18, 1805, Captain Clark took 11 men, including his servant York, and traveled west to see this great sight.

They ventured several miles up the coastline on the Washington side of the river. Here for the first time, they had the opportunity to see the mighty Pacific Ocean. It had been a long and hard trip, but what joy must have been felt by the men to realize the journey was over.

Upon Captain Clark's return, he joined Captain Lewis in a meeting with several Chinooks Chiefs. One of the Chiefs had a robe of sea otter skins, which both Captains admired. The skins were the most beautiful they had ever seen. All attempts to purchase this prize robe were to no avail, as the Chief wanted only blue beads in trade.

The Chief pointed to the blue beaded belt Sacagawea wore around her waist. This was a prize possession of hers, perhaps given to her by her Shoshoni mother. Would she be willing to part with it so the Captains could obtain this robe? It is not known whether she gave this up willingly or if the Captains pressured her. However, the belt was given to the Chief. Perhaps Captain Clark wanted this beautiful robe to present to his intended finance when he returned home? It would certainly make an outstanding present for any fortunate lady.

Sacagawea received a blue cloth coat in return for her selfless sacrifice. It was made of wool and kept her warm and dry.

The expedition was at the end of the trail to the Pacific Northwest. The men had accomplished what President Jefferson had expected of them; they had mapped a route to the Pacific coast. Although they had not found a Northwest Passage by river, they had proved that such a journey across the land was possible. Now it was time to settle on a place to winter over, and to build protection from the wet weather.

The Clatsop, who resided on the south side of the Columbia River, had informed the expedition there was an abundance of game on that side. At this point, the Captains decide to give everyone a chance to vote on whether to stay where they were for the winter, go back upriver to a place near the Sandy River, or to cross to the other side of the river and settle there for the winter.

Everyone voted, including York and Sacagawea. Sacagawea became the first woman and Native American to cast a vote in what is now the United States. Her vote was cast to go where there were many roots and berries for food.

York, Captain Clark's servant, an African American, was also given the privilege of voting. This is a very historic vote in the history of our country. He voted to cross the river.

The majority of votes were cast to cross the Columbia and build their living quarters on the south side of the river. Once there, the men quickly engaged in building Fort Clatsop, named after the local Native American Nation. How wonderful for Sacagawea and all the men to have solid shelter, and a place to get out of the rain and cold wind. There she could better protect and care for her child, Jean Baptiste.

The expedition stayed at Fort Clatsop for almost four months, from December 1805, to March 1806, and it is recorded that only 12 days did it not rain and there were only six days when they could see the sun.

The expedition was low on supplies, so the hunters went out almost every day to kill elk and deer, bringing them back to the fort. However, they had run out of salt to cure the meat, and the meat was spoiling rapidly due to the wet weather.

Captain Lewis directed five men to engage in the process of extracting salt from sea water. Private Joseph Field had gleaned some knowledge of the process when he had observed his brother Ezekial working at a salt plant in Kentucky. Also accompanying Private Joseph Field were Privates George Gibson and William Bratton. These three men were charged with the task of gathering salt from the sea. Accompanying them were Privates William Werner and Alexander Willard.

The party left Fort Clatsop and headed west to begin their task. They had five large kettles in which to boil sea water. Salt water is heaver than fresh water, and since they were near the mouth of the Columbia, where fresh water was flowing into the ocean, it was necessary to travel approximately 15 miles from the fort to find a place where the water had an acceptable concentration of salt.

After testing the water in several places along the shore, they finally found the ideal spot. Not only was the water high in salt content, but the place was near a small Clatsop and Nehalem Indian village. There were an abundance of rocks to build an open pit for the fire, and plenty of timber to burn.

The men extracted approximately three quarts to a gallon of salt per day. Three men were constantly at work boiling a total of approximately 1400 gallons of seawater. This procedure continued

24 hours a day, 7 days a week, for 2½ months. The salt was pure white and of fine quality. During this period of time, approximately 3½ bushels of salt was produced.

On February 20, 1806, the saltmakers' camp was abandoned and the men returned to the fort. This amount of salt was sufficient for their stay at Fort Clatsop and they had a plentiful supply for the journey home. The site of the saltmakers camp is located in Seaside, Oregon and is now included in the Lewis and Clark National Park sites.

Back at Fort Clatsop, the men were busy hunting while Sacagawea was finding roots and some berries to supplement their daily food supply. Although they did not have a great deal of food, they lived as well as could be expected in this new land.

In January, 1806, the Native Americans informed Captain Clark that across the mountain, now called Tillamook Head, a great fish had washed up on the beach. Here was an opportunity for them to supplement their food supply by obtaining whale blubber and oil.

As soon as the weather permitted, Captain Clark arranged for a party of 12 men to travel to this site. Upon hearing of this, Sacagawea asked to travel with the party. At first Captain Clark refused her request. However, Sacagawea became quite insistent on going with the men. This is the first instance of Sacagawea making a request in a very strong manner.

In broken English and sign language, she informed the Captain that she had come all this way, providing food for the men and helping them in any way she could, and it was not fair that she could not go to see the mighty waters and this very large fish. Approximately 24 months of hardships and travel, and Sacagawea had not yet seen the ocean and she begged to accompany the men to see the wondrous sight.

Finally, Captain Clark relented and the party included Charbonneau, Sacagawea, and Jean Baptiste. They left the following day and when they stopped at the Saltmakers' Camp, Sacagawea had the opportunity to look upon the Pacific Ocean for the first time.

What her feelings were as she beheld this magnificent body of water are not recorded, but imagine the thoughts going through her mind. A young Shoshoni girl from the mid-west sees the immense ocean with gray winter waves crashing on the never-ending shore. In the middle of winter, the ocean is usually stormy, with great waves and swells breaking as far as the eye can see.

When the party finally crossed Tillamook Head, there was the great fish, but all that was left was the skeleton. According to Captain Clark, it measured 105 feet long. The Native Americans had taken the meat, but Captain Clark was able to trade for 300 pounds of blubber and some whale oil. Again there is no record of what went through Sacagawea's mind as she beheld what was left of this great fish. The place where the fish washed ashore is now called Ecola, meaning whale or great fish in the Clatsop language.

When the saltmakers returned to Fort Clatsop, with approximately 3½ bushels of sea salt, the men were busy making preparations to leave the west coast and return home. New clothes and moccasins were essential. The men and Sacagawea made approximately 358 pairs of moccasins while they were at Fort Clatsop. Moccasins lasted only a few weeks on the trail, and Sacagawea was busy making clothes for Charbonneau, Jean Baptiste and herself.

Jean Baptiste, like all young children, was growing by leaps and bounds and seemed to be rapidly outgrowing his clothes. Making his clothes was in addition to Sacagawea's other duties, such as gathering roots for the men to eat, and assisting in dressing the hides from the elk and deer the men shot.

Sacagawea's son, Jean Baptiste, celebrated his first birthday while at Fort Clatsop. He was fascinated by Private Cruzatte's fiddle and the music. When the men were gathered around the fort in the evening, and the music was playing, Jean Baptiste often danced. Captain Clark referred to Jean Baptiste as "his little dancing boy."

The vision of this small dancing boy must have given the men quite a bit of pleasure. Here was a glimpse of home and family that the men were missing.

On March 23, 1806, the decision was made to leave Fort Clatsop and begin the trek home. The fort was dedicated to the Clatsop Nation. A letter was posted with the names of the men who had undertaken this great journey. As Sacagawea was not an official member of the expedition, her name was not mentioned on this posting.

Sacagawea must have felt a great sense of relief to be returning to the Mandan village. What tales she would have to tell all the people. She had certainly seen sights that no one in her village or tribe had ever witnessed.

Jean Baptiste had grown much during the time. He was learning how to talk and this was a marvelous opportunity for Sacagawea and Charbonneau to teach him new words. He would be taught Shoshoni, Hidatsa and French language, so he could function in all three societies.

# CHAPTER 6

# HOME
# TO THE MANDANS

ON APRIL 27, 1806, the expedition returned to the Wallawallas
and the country of Chief Yellept. This was a village of around 150
men, about 12 miles below the junction of the Columbia and the
Snake Rivers on the north bank. Here once again, Sacagawea's
abilities are tested and found to be indeed adequate.

There was a captive Shoshoni woman with the Wallawallas,
and with Sacagawea's help the woman could converse and give
the men information about a shortcut at the end of Lolo Trail.
Once again the interpretation went from Sacagawea to Charbonneau in Hidatsa, then to Drouillard or LaBiche in French, then to
the Captains in English. As difficult as this was, it was extremely
effective and without the services of Sacagawea, it would have
been almost impossible.

After leaving the Wallawallas, on May 22, 1806, Jean Baptiste
became seriously ill. This was a most frightening event. He had
retained good health all during the trip thus far, which was a

tribute to his mother's skills and his own strong disposition.

But in late May, his jaw and throat were greatly swollen. For two days, the expedition halted while the Captains applied poultices to the effected area. Both Captains were up all night with Jean Baptiste until he recovered. In modern day medical terms, he probably suffered an abscess or mastoiditis. The anguish that Sacagawea must have been felt for her child was undoubtedly great, but with supreme confidence she placed her son's welfare in the hands of the Captains and allowed them to treat her child.

Sacagawea's reactions to Jean Baptiste's illness are not recorded in the journals, but apparently both Captains were extremely concerned about this situation, and treated the child with great care and tenderness. Sacagawea undoubtedly felt great relief when Jean Baptiste recovered and once again enjoyed good health. Her gratitude to the Captains for all of their help was enormous.

After this harrowing experience, the expedition continued. By this time, Jean Baptiste was developing his own personality, and endearing himself to all the men.

Captain Clark was so fond of Jean Baptiste that he gave him the nickname of "Pomp." Later on in the summer, Captain Clark named a stone monolith "Pompy's Tower." It is now called "Pompeys Pillar," and is a national monument, located 25 miles east of present day Billings, Montana. This is a fitting memorial for the youngest person of the expedition.

On the journey home, the expedition encountered tribes that had taken Shoshoni prisoners. Sacagawea was asked to translate for these tribes as she was the only one who could understand this language. Again, her helpfulness and abilities was a tremendous asset to the expedition.

The expedition stopped at the same Nez Perce village and rested. Here the Captains again treated various ailments of the people. The Captains had treated one of their own men, Private Bratton, with sweat baths when he could not walk or sit up without pain. This proved a successful method for this ailment.

One of the Native Americans brought his father to the Captains. This man had not been able to walk or use his arms for approximately five years. After repeated sweats, full movements of his limbs were restored. He was extremely grateful to the Captains for all their help. The Captains were quite impressed by the love and respect these young men showed for the older generation.

The men rounded up their branded horses to continue their journey home. All of the horses, plus a few new colts were found safe and sound.

On August 17, 1806, the Charbonneau family prepared to leave the expedition and once again resume their lives among the Mandans. Captain Lewis's comments in the journals were not extremely complimentary about Charbonneau's abilities during the journey. He inferred only that Charbonneau was good as an interpreter and usually did his duties with good intentions.

Captain Clark was sadden at the prospect of having to leave Jean Baptiste behind, and conveyed to the family that he wished to take the boy with him. He promised to raise the child as his own, giving him the best education and every advantage possible so he would be prepared to enter the world as a highly educated young man.

It was agreed between the Charbonneaus and Captain Clark that when Jean Baptiste was weaned, the couple would take him to Captain Clark in St. Louis. This was indeed a wonderful opportunity for Jean Baptiste. It also illustrates the unselfishness of Sacagawea. She was willing to give up her only child so he would have all the opportunities of being educated according to the standards of white people.

Charbonneau was paid for his services and promised 360 acres of land near St. Louis if he decided to settle there. Captain Clark mentions, with regret, he is unable to reimburse Sacagawea for all her assistance. He praises Sacagawea highly for all she has done to insure the success of the expedition.

The Charbonneau family settled back into life in the Mandan village. Jean Baptiste was raised with other children and Sacagawea reflected on all she had seen and learned. What tales she had to tell her people. She had seen grizzly bears, elks, deer, and huge rattlesnakes, great bodies of water, many different tribes, large forests and shiny mountains.

Sacagawea had accomplished much in her short lifetime. Her many qualities were vital to the success of the expedition. She was much more than a guide and the expedition would not have made it to the Pacific Northwest and back without her help. She deserves to be well remembered for her patience, calmness, composure, unselfishness, persistence and perseverance. She was indeed a very remarkable woman.

# CHAPTER 7

# MARIE DORION

IN 1814, Marie walked, stumbled, and crawled along the snow-covered ground. She had left her two boys under a makeshift shelter with nothing but a buffalo robe to protect them from the winter weather. Neither the two boys nor Marie had had much to eat for at least six days.

Marie had seen smoke in the distance and she thought if she could reach the smoke, she and her sons would be safe. But what would happen if this was not a friendly village?

When Marie could go no farther, she rested in the snow. Her thoughts went back to the circumstances that have led up to this desperate situation...

Marie Dorion was an Iowa Native American. She became the second Native American woman to cross the country. She was born around 1786, about the same time as Sacagawea. She spent the early part of her life living near the Red River Country in Arkansas. There is little historical information about her early childhood.

Marie would have learned about the traditions of her people and survival skills.

Pierre Dorion Jr. was French Canadian on his father's side and Sioux on his mother's side. One historical fact states that Pierre had taken another woman, Holy Rainbow, for his wife. He apparently left her and then chose Marie for his new wife.

This was not a match made in heaven, as Pierre had a volatile temper and often was abusive.

Marie was quite capable of defending herself, and she did not take this abuse in a passive manner. There are many tales of her knocking Pierre out with one good punch, thus putting an end to his poor behavior.

This rather strange union produced two boys, Baptiste and Paul. Paul was reported to have been born with an affliction and at age two could not walk or sit up. This made it very difficult for Marie, as she had to carry him in a sling at all times.

Pierre Jr. was an excellent guide and hunter. He provided quite well for his family. He had little difficulty in obtaining jobs when he was sober, however, his drinking binges made work spasmodic and oftentimes there were great stretches between periods of employment.

Manual Lisa, who was a well-known fur trader, had hired

Pierre to work for his company. Knowing Pierre's fondness for liquor, one evening Lisa took advantage of him and allowed the liquor to flow quite freely. After an all night drinking binge, and giving free drinks to all of his friends, Pierre was informed that he and his friends consumed $300 of whiskey.

This was around a year's salary for Pierre, and Lisa demanded payment. Lisa was willing to take this amount out of Pierre's pay that he was to receive for a trapping expedition. Marie felt Lisa had taken advantage of Pierre, and she was willing to leave Arkansas and go to St. Louis where there would be other opportunities for Pierre to work.

Once in St Louis, Marie learned that Sacagawea, Charbonneau, and Jean Baptiste were also in St. Louis. Captain Clark had promised Charbonneau land and money to start his own farming business and the Charbonneaus had arrived to start a new way of life.

Marie had heard of Sacagawea's journey to the west coast with Lewis and Clark. Pierre Dorion Sr. had worked for a short period of time for the Captains as a guide and interpreter. Because of the close connection to the Clark family, the Charbonneaus were held in great respect. Marie hoped that Pierre would also be in a position to command respect, and she saw the chance for him to gain stature with the Astor Party.

# CHAPTER 8

# THE ASTORIANS

IN 1810, John Jacob Astor, a New York financier, was planning to establish a fur trading business at the mouth of the Columbia River. Astor had already chosen the man who would lead this expedition across the country: Wilson Price Hunt. Hunt needed a few experienced men to accompany him and the 60 men who were selected to make this journey. Most of the men Hunt had already chosen were engineers and clerks, so it was very important to have an individual who had knowledge of trading, trapping and survival skills.

Pierre had excellent skills in these areas and he also saw a way to get out from under the debt he owed to Lisa. Hunt signed Pierre to be their guide. Marie was most anxious to make the journey with them, as she knew Pierre would have to stay sober during this trip. Hunt did his best to convenience Pierre the trip would be too hard on Marie and the boys, but Pierre was adamant that Marie and the children accompany them. Hunt finally agreed to this arrangement. Perhaps Hunt was aware of how important Sacagawea had been to Lewis and Clark and felt Marie Dorion might have the same value to his party of travelers.

Pierre then confided to Marie he did not intend to work for either Hunt or Lisa. His plan was take the $200 Hunt had paid him in advance money, leave St. Louis, return when things died down, and then look for another position. Marie would not consent to this type of cheating, and insisted Pierre keep his word. Following another fight between the two, Marie took her belongings, the two boys, and left Pierre.

When Pierre woke the next morning and found his family gone, he quickly joined the Hunt party thinking Marie would be with them. But Marie was not to be found. After a search by some crew members which turned up no trace of Marie, Pierre spent the evening in self-pity for his rash actions towards his family.

The next morning, Marie was seen on the banks of the Missouri river, and a canoe was sent to pick her up with the two boys and return them to the boat.

The Hunt party, including the Dorian's, departed on their long journey. Of the 60 men, only 45 would reach their destination.

Hunt was eager to leave St. Louis, as he did not want to have any trouble with Lisa over hiring Pierre as the guide. However, it was impossible to avoid Lisa and his trapping and hunting party. Hunt and Lisa had both learned that the Blackfeet had joined the Sioux Nations and were becoming quite troublesome to all the hunting parties traveling the Missouri River. As the Lisa party was smaller and less encumbered by baggage, they quickly caught up with the Hunt party. It was convenient for the two parties to travel together, as this provided strength in numbers.

Sacagawea and Charbonneau were traveling with the Lisa

party. They were going to stay at Fort Manual, and Charbonneau would do trapping for Lisa. Although the Charbonneaus were grateful to Captain Clark for his offer to give them a start in farming, they realized that life in the city was not for them. They were frontier people and yearned to return to the west.

What an opportunity for Marie to meet Sacagawea and learn from her personally of the trials and triumphs of the cross country journey. During the evening, when the boats were docked along the river bank, Marie went to the Charbonneau's tent to talk with Sacagawea.

Both women were pregnant at this time, although Marie had not revealed her condition to Hunt. The Charbonneaus had left Jean Baptiste in St. Louis with Captain Clark, where he would start his education. Perhaps the sight of Marie's two sons was a reminder to Sacagawea what she had given up for her son.

The women met a few times during this short period and this would be the last opportunity Marie would have to talk with a woman for nearly a year.

Through sign language, broken French, and some words of English, the two women were able to converse and Marie learned much from Sacagawea concerning the land she was to see.

When it was time to again start their journey, Hunt decided to no longer follow the maps provided by Captain Clark, but to go south in order to avoid the Sioux. These maps had been revised by George Drouillard, a guide for the Lewis and Clark expedition, as he had visited Captain Clark in 1809, and provided improved maps. All Hunt had to do was follow the existing path and the journey would have been accomplished with fewer lives lost and the men would not have suffered so much from hunger and exposure.

From here on, the Astorians, as they called themselves, would have numerous troubles on the journey. None of this was Pierre's fault, but all rested on the faulty decisions made by Hunt.

The party now entered into unknown territory, and Pierre was called on to use all his skills. It was necessary for him to find game, water for the men, and good grazing land for the horses. Pierre was up to this task, and proved his worth to the party. For all of the trouble Pierre had caused in the beginning, Hunt soon realized how valuable this man would be on the journey.

Marie walked or rode the horse assigned to her. It was her duty to keep an eye on the boys and keep them out of trouble and not to interfere with the men or get in their way. She showed no sign of having any difficulty in keeping up with the men, even though her pregnancy was now showing, and she found it necessary to carry Paul in a sling much of the time. Marie's uncomplaining attitude and disposition set an example for all the men to follow. No one dared complain about the arduous journey or the hardships they were enduring.

By mid-September, they crossed the Grand Tetons, and by October 8, 1811, they were close to present day St. Anthony, Idaho. There were still plenty of provisions. It could have been easy to be in Astoria in a few months from this location.

But once again Hunt did not show strong leadership. The voyageurs insisted on building 13 dugout canoes for the ride down the Snake River. Valuable days were lost in this endeavor. The river was swollen with rain and dangerous to navigate at this point.

Seventy horses were left with some Shoshonis and the party transferred to the dugouts. Soon the smooth sailing changed, and the river plunged through steep canyons and produced many rapids.

At one point, it took all the strength of the boatmen to prevent the dugouts from being sucked into a whirlpool. The first dugout and second made it safely to shore, but the third one did not succeed. Ramsey Crooks, and one of the oarsmen, managed to stay afloat to be rescued, but one of the other French Canadians, Clappine, was sucked under the water and not seen again.

Marie must have been very grateful when Hunt became convinced they could not continue to travel by water. The rough rapids were frightening enough for the men, but Marie had to hold on to her boys, so they would not be swept overboard. This must have been very upsetting to her, but again she uttered no complaints about the situation.

Hunt sent three men back to where they had left their horses with instructions to return with the animals. After a few days, the men returned and informed Hunt that they could not reach the place where the horses were in time to be of assistance to the party.

At this point, Hunt divided the party into smaller groups, so they would have a better chance of survival. Now, each member of the party would have to carry approximately 20 pounds of equipment, and food, while continuing the journey on foot.

The men Hunt had sent on ahead to determine if they could travel by river had returned and informed them the river was to treacherous to navigate. It was too early in the year to take the river route.

Hunt had command of the main party, consisting of 31 men and the Dorions. Before they could leave this spot, they had to bury the baggage and merchandise which Hunt decided to leave. Here was another difficult task required of Marie.

The journey on foot was tortuous, including steep climbs and rough rocks. Many nights, the men were exhausted, due to this very rugged terrain and lack of food.

Finally Pierre was able to trade some items for a horse Marie and the boys could ride. How welcome this must have been to Marie, as she was quite weary.

After the party split up, Hunt spotted some of the men across the river, and managed to send across some food. The men were starving, being unable to kill any game. One of the men, Prevost, was in the boat that had travelled across the river, and when it also capsized, Marie again saw a fellow traveler disappear beneath the waters.

Once again Hunt had the party broken up into smaller groups. At this point, some of the men made the decision to winter in that spot and in the spring head for Astoria. Pierre continued with Hunt. Hunt requested Pierre to kill Marie's horse, so the men could have food. Pierre refused this request, although Hunt was adamant about the situation. Surprisingly enough, Pierre proved to be a caring husband, and decided Marie needed the horse to carry her and the baby once it was born.

In the middle of December, a small dugout was sent across the river to bring the men of one of the other groups to the side where Hunt's party was and the two groups combined. By now they were near the Powder River in Grand Ronde Valley in Eastern Oregon.

The time had come for Marie to give birth to her child. The men were concerned for her, as her good conduct and persistence had earned their goodwill.

Pierre treated it as just another occurrence. He left the party with Marie and the two boys, and assured Hunt they would rejoin them by the next day.

Marie gave birth to an infant who was born prematurely. Marie had little milk to nurse, and the baby was very weak. As Pierre was part French Canadian, historians have listed this new born as the first white child born in the Oregon Territory.

The next day, the Dorions rejoined the party. Marie had the infant in her arms and a sling carrying Paul at her side. She had endured all the hardships the men had endured, and many more.

On January 6, they crossed over the summit of the Blue Mountains and could see the Columbia River plains. This gave them great hope the journey would soon end.

By now the snow was melting and they could see tracks of black-tailed deer and Native American hunters. Many of the men dropped back as hunger and fatigue keep them from keeping up with the party, but Marie plodded on with her children.

On January 7, the infant Marie had tried so valiantly to feed and nourish passed away and was buried along the trail. Pierre dug a small grave and put rocks on top so wild animals could not get to it. The location is near North Powder, Oregon. He remembered a prayer he had learned as a youth and recited it over the grave, and they mourned the loss of their child.

How sad this must have been for Marie. She had struggled so long and hard to protect all of her family, but in the end was unable to save the precious new life. There is no record that any of the events surrounding the birth and death of the infant slowed or delayed the party of Astorians, and Marie kept up with the men and continued to be assistance in her time of grief.

Shortly thereafter, they reached a Native American village, where they were able to trade for some meat and roots. Here

Marie cooked a meal for all of them, and temporarily they were satisfied. The stragglers came into camp and were grateful to have food. Horses could be purchased for a blanket, or some blue beads, and the party once again became well-equipped to finish their journey.

After a few days of rest, the party continued on. They crossed the Columbia River, and the party was near the end of this incredibly difficult trip. The Hunt party reached Astoria on February 15, 1812. Here they were warmly welcomed by one of the smaller groups that had separated from the main party months before.

How welcoming the sight of this small but well-built fort must have been to travel-weary Marie. Now at last, she could rest, have food, and care for her husband and two boys. This would be their home for the next year. Then Marie and her boys would face the biggest test of endurance and hardships imaginable. Nothing that Marie had gone through before would be equal to what was to come in the future.

For now, things became a little easier for this hard-working woman. While Pierre was assigned to hunt and trap food for all the Astorians, Marie was busy making clothes for her family, preparing food for storage, and sewing moccasins to be sold at the fort. This assisted in paying for the supplies, such as vegetables seeds, flour, and some staples. With these, Marie and her family would be assured of having ample food to eat.

Marie lived a good life at Fort Astoria, compared to the life she had lived on the trail. By now, the men had spread her story of survival and composure to everyone. They told of the birth and death of her child, and how she persevered. Marie became a well-known and respected person.

# CHAPTER 9

# SURVIVAL
# AND TRIUMPH

**IN THE SUMMER OF 1813,** Pierre was given a new assignment. John Reed was appointed head of a trapping party that was to settle near the Boise River, and Pierre was to go along and be responsible for the trapping. This meant Marie and the two boys would give up their home at Fort Astoria and once again face life in the wilderness.

The Reed party traveled up the Columbia River to Umatilla. Marie tried to persuade Reed, through her husband, to go overland as this would be a shorter route and they would have the ability to set up their winter headquarters much quicker. However, Reed did not heed Marie's advice and followed the Snake River to its confluence with the Clearwater River. This action once again delayed the endeavors of the Astorians.

Eventually near Caldwell, Idaho, the group set up headquarters. However, this was a less than desirable location, as the Native Americans in that area were not friendly. The group moved a

few a miles east, established a second hut, and here Marie resided with her two boys.

Pierre and two other men went ahead, about two or three days journey, and established their hunting and trapping camp. The trapping was very good and Pierre returned to the second hut, with numerous pelts. It was Marie's duty to prepare the meals, dress the pelts, make and repair clothes for all individuals and take care of her two boys.

All went well for a few months, until one evening in January,

1814, a friendly Native American informed Marie that some Dog-Rib Snake Indians had burned the first hut the group had constructed and were now headed for the camp where Pierre and his men were. The Native Americans were armed and chanting war songs.

Marie decided to warn her husband of this possible attack. She put the two boys on a horse, and went in search of Pierre and his men. After a few days of riding, she spotted smoke ahead.

Frightened and upset by the eerie silence all around them, Marie paused, not knowing what she would find. It was unusual not to hear the men conversing with one another, not to hear the clanging of the beaver traps. Suddenly, she heard a noise in the trees in front of her.

Marie held on to her knife in case it was an unfriendly Native American. Instead it was one of the men, LeClere, who was badly wounded and bleeding. He informed Marie that the men have been attacked and robbed that morning. Pierre and the two other men were killed instantly and their bodies mutilated.

Marie did not go into the hut, as she realized there was nothing she could do for her husband. A noise startled both her and LeClere. Thinking it might be the unfriendly Natives, they hid among the trees. However, horses the Dog-Rib Indians had left were making the noise and Marie was able to secure another horse for their ride back to safety.

LeClere was a big man, but Marie managed to lift him up on one of the horses. She put her son Paul up with him. Marie rode the other horse with her other son Baptiste and they started out for the second hut. Not too many miles later they heard the noise of horses and men. Hiding in the woods, they could see the Dog-Rib Indians.

Fortunately, they were not spotted, and the Indians continued on their way. LeClere fell off his horse and opened up his wounds, and passed away during the night. Marie covered the body with bushes and snow. She had no choice but to bury him there and continued on to what she thought would be a safe place.

However, when she arrived at the second hut, again she found tragedy. Reed and his men had all been killed. Their bodies had been mutilated and every possible means of torture the Dog-Ribs could think of had been committed on their bodies. The post had been ransacked and destroyed.

Now Marie was truly alone, surrounded by unfriendly Natives. She had to protect her boys from suffering the same fate that had befallen the men. After a long, cold, and hungry night spent in the woods, Marie assessed her situation. Once again, all of Marie's survival skills came into use. She remembered there was a great deal of fish stored near the post. Leaving the boys wrapped in buffalo robes, in a makeshift shelter, and under cover of darkness, she went in search of that food.

Marie found deer robes and dried fish. She returned to the boys, and although it was dangerous, she built a small fire, cooked some of the fish, and they had their first meal in three days.

After two trips to gather more fish, Marie collapsed and was unable to move for a few days. When she recovered, she packed her small possessions on the horses, gathered up the two boys and started toward Astoria and safety.

They crossed the Snake River, and continued in a northwesterly direction, always on the lookout for unfriendly Natives and wild animals.

Finally, the horses could not go any farther, due to lack of food, so she slaughtered both horses and built a small fire to cook the horse meat. Their hides were used for warmth in the cold, hostile country. Marie selected a spot near a stream, and constructed a hut, primarily of branches and whatever she could gather from the area.

Marie had a knife, and with this she was able to cut wood for fuel. In this lonely, desolate, hut, she and her two boys spent 53 days. She never knew if the unfriendly Natives were close by or if they had left the area. She dared not venture too far from this shelter. She was the only hope the boys had to make it out of this situation alive. When the food ran low, and Marie thought there was a break in the weather, she and the boys left their hut and continued on toward the Blue Mountains.

After a few days of travel, Marie suffered from snow blindness and was unable to continue. Snow blindness is extremely painful and it must have been unnerving for the boys to see their mother suffer.

But Marie recovered and she and the boys crossed the Blue Mountains on foot. They were not able to cover great distances daily, only about two or three miles, due to the cold weather and the ongoing hunger.

The overriding fact that drove Marie to continue on this incredible journey was the safety of her two boys. She was all that stood between them and certain death in this cold, forsaken place. Marie needed to gather all of her strength and skills to take the boys to safety. By now the food was running low.

Marie saw smoke in the distance, which indicated a village. She knew her only chance of survival was to reach that village. But would it be a friendly village? That was a chance Marie had to take.

She placed her boys in a shelter surrounded by two logs, covered with snow, and wrapped in buffalo robes. Then she started toward the smoke. They had had little food in the last six days, and Marie stumbled, crawled, and dragged herself towards the village. She dared not to think of what the circumstances would be if this were an unfriendly village. When she was too hungry and exhausted to go on, and she fell into a deep sleep.

Awaking, she continued her tortuous journey, and finally reached the Walla Walla River and followed it for about three hours. By noon, she reached the village of the friendly Walla Walla. She managed to tell the people about her two boys and some men left immediately to find them. It was easy to tell where they were, as all they had to do was to follow the path Marie had left in the snow.

When they returned to the village, Marie was grateful to learn that her sons had survived. Marie must have instilled in the boys some of her courage and fortitude for them to have managed to stay alive within that small shelter while she was away. What a remarkable feat for the boys who were now eight and six years old.

It is estimated the entire journey that Marie and the boys traveled from Idaho to the Walla Walla village was over 260 miles. The Walla Wallas left them to rest, have some food, and regain their health. In spite of all Marie had been through, she regained her health rapidly and insisted she go to the nearby Columbia River, to wait on the shore, where she might encounter some of the Astorians.

Marie felt the Astorians would be coming up the river to check on Reed and his party. There was a small village where she and boys stayed and about a month later, she spotted canoes bearing James Keith and a party of Astorians.

Keith had orders to check on the Reed party. In broken English and some French, Marie told of the tragedy of Reed and all the men. Her incredible trials were recorded at that time in journals by two of the party members. After recovering from the shock of this gruesome tale, they were deeply grateful Marie and the boys had survived their ordeal.

Immediately, they wanted Marie and the boys to join them in the journey back to St. Louis. However, Marie declined this offer. After gathering the boys, they took her to Fort Okanogan, situated on the Columbia River, in eastern Washington. This was a trading post owned by the North West Fur Company and here Marie and the boys could stay. Now the journey of hardship and near starvation was over.

Marie's story quickly spread around the country, and many of the mountain men commented that they doubted if they themselves could have survived such an ordeal. Marie quickly became a legend around many campfires. In the book "The Astorians," by Washington Irving, he recounted Marie's entire heroic journey.

# CHAPTER 10

# MARIE'S NEW LIFE

WHILE AT FORT OKANOGAN, Marie set up housekeeping. She kept busy making moccasins to sell at the fort, as she had done at Fort Astoria. With this trade item, she was able to purchase needed food and supplies for her family. Her loneliness must have been incredible. Although Pierre had not been a perfect mate, at times when he was sober, he was kind and loving to the boys, and apparently devoted to Marie. He had proven his devotion when he refused to slaughter her horse when they were traveling with Hunt.

It would be extremely difficult for Marie to raise her sons without a father. The husbands or men of the families provided necessary protection for the women, and guidance in raising male children. If the father was not able to do this, the task was taken up by brothers or uncles. As Marie did not have family in this place, who would step in to teach Baptiste and Paul all the many skills they would need? Marie could certainly teach survival skills as well as any man, but with her household duties, where would she find the time?

Marie was not to be left alone. At the fort she found companionship with Louis Joseph Venier. The marriage was most likely a tribal ceremony, and this union produced a daughter, Marguerite. Now Marie had three children, and from all accounts, she had a good marriage to Louis. However, Louis was soon killed by hostile Native Americans and once again Marie was alone with three children to care for and watch over.

A few years after the death of Louis Venier, Marie became reacquainted with Jean Baptiste Toupin who was employed at Fort Walla Walla. Jean Toupin had known the Dorions in St. Louis. He was of French Canadian and Native American decent. Jean had worked for the Hudson's Bay Company and had heard of Marie's outstanding deeds. After a short acquaintance, Marie and Jean were married by a tribal ceremony and by all accounts, they were very happy.

After Jean's service to the Hudson's Bay Company ended, the Toupins moved to what was then called the French Prairie. This was the Willamette Valley in Oregon, where many of the French Canadians, along with their Native American wives, had settled. This union, between Jean and Marie produced a son, Francis or Francois, and a daughter, Marie Anne.

Marie now had a nice home and was able to take care of her family. There was no more hunger or extreme cold weather to contend with. Marie became a well-respected woman. She was known for her willingness to assist any family in need, and take care of children who became orphans. She became a leader of the women.

Narcissa Whitman spoke of meeting Marie on Marie's visit to Waiilatpu in the spring of 1838. It is also thought that Marie played a part in the release of the hostages taken by the Cayuse

Indians after the Whitman massacre.

By now there was a Catholic Church in St. Paul, Oregon. Marie was taking instruction in the Catholic religion and was in great demand in assisting with translations of the Native American languages to French and English. She became quite active in the Catholic Church and was an inspiration to all the women in the community. Once again, Marie's leadership qualities were in great demand. Marie never backed down from a challenge and enjoyed a very full life in the French Prairie.

Jean and Marie had lived together 18 years before their marriage was legitimatized. They were married in the Catholic Church in St. Paul, Oregon, on July 19, 1841, and she and all of her children living at home were baptized. At this time, it was estimated that Marie was 51 year of age. Jean Baptiste was now 34, Paul was 32, Marguerite was 21, Francois 17, and Marie Anne 14 years of age. The fact that they had lived together for 18 years before they were married was acceptable as there were not priests or churches in the early days of this settlement.

Baptiste, her oldest son, had also married and his children were baptized at the same time as he and Marie.

When talking of her children, Marie mentioned she had another son, Paul, who had a big mouth that stretched almost from ear to ear, and very small eyes. She stated he had run off with some friendly Native Americans a while ago, and she did not know where he was. It is not known if Marie every saw Paul again.

Marie and Jean lived a very productive and useful life and on September 5, 1850, Marie passed away. She had been given the title "Madam Dorion". As none of her husbands had held high position in the country, the title "Madam Dorion" was awarded to her for all of the contributions she had made during her lifetime. She is the only Native American woman to be given this title.

However, when Marie was called Madame Dorion, she often corrected people and stated that her name was Marie Toupin. She was also called Marie Iowa, and by adding the prefix" la" to this tribal name, in French she was called Marie La Guivoise.

After her passing, she was buried under the steeple of the parish church in St. Louis, Oregon. This is usually a place of honor reserved for a high church official, and it shows what great respect Marie commanded in her later life. Her force of character, bravery, love, caring, compassion, kindness and helpfulness are all qualities that make this woman well worth remembering. She was truly a heroine.

Marie outlived Sacagawea and Watkuese, although all three were born at approximately the same time. Sacagawea passed away December 20, 1812 at Fort Manual. Her passing is recorded by the clerk at the fort, John Luttig. He writes, "This evening the wife of Charbonneau, A Snake squaw, died of putrid fever. She was a good and the best woman in the fort, aged about 25 years. She left a fine infant girl."[9]

The young daughter of Sacagawea and Charbonneau, named Lizette, was taken to St. Louis by John Luttig, and was also raised by Captain Clark. There is not much known about her, and is thought she passed away at age 10 from a high fever.

All three of these Native American women were extremely courageous, and deserve a place in our history books as brave, un-complaining women, who overcame unbelievable odds. Without

---

[9] Susan M. Colby, *Sacagawea's Child*, Spokane, Washington, The Arthur H. Clark Company, page 86

their valiant efforts, the course of our history would be written in an entirely different manner.

We need to honor these very valiant women and never forget the sacrifices they made for our country. Sacagawea's love of adventure; Watkuese's love of her people and homeland; and Maria Dorion's love for her children. All three Native American women expressed this never ending love in everything they did. This love was the enduring quality that gave them the courage to continue on under unbelievable circumstances. They are true heroines indeed.

# EPILOGUE

IN MANY WAYS, I feel like I have "lived" with these three women for the past year while I have been doing research for this book. They have become my best friends. That is the reason I have tried very hard not to fictionalize their stories. In my opinion, their stories are dramatic and compelling enough, without embellishment.

If Watkuese had not uttered her four words, "Do them no harm" Lewis and Clark and the entire expedition might have been slaughtered at that point. Great Britain, Russia and Spain were all trying to establish ownership in the Pacific Northwest, to control the fur trading. Would our area of this country now be under a foreign flat?

Without Sacagawea's help in translating Shoshoni into Hidatsa language, would Lewis and Clark have been able to secure horses and continue their journey?

Without Marie Dorion's persistence, would the Astorians have survived on their incredible journey?

These three Native American women deserve to be honored for all their heroic deeds. They are entitled to a place of respect in the history of our country. Without their help, our country's history at that period of time may have been written with a very different ending.

# BIBLIOGRAPHY

Ambrose, Stephen E., "Undaunted Courage," New York, N.Y:
Simon & Schuster, 1996

Colby, Susan M., "Sacagawea's Child," Spokane, Washington:
the Arthur H. Clark Company, 2005

Halfmoon, Otis, "Discovering Lewis and Clark," Washburn,
North Dakota: The Lewis & Clark Fort Mandan Foundation, 2009

Huffman, Molly, "The Lewis & Clark Saltmakers of Seaside,"
Seaside, Oregon: Seaside Museum & Historical Society

Irving, Washington, "Astoria," Middlesex, TW: The Echo Library, 1897

McWhorter, L. V., "Hear Me, My Chiefs!  Nez Perce Legend &
History". Caldwell, Idaho: Caxton Press, 2001

Moulton, Gary E., "The Definitive Journals of Lewis & Clark."
Volumes 3, 4, 5, 6,  Lincoln, Nebraska, The University of Nebraska
Press, 1988

Peltier, Jerome, "Madame Dorion," Fairfield, Washington: Ye Galleon
Press, 1980

Ronda, James P., "Lewis & Clark Among The Indians," Lincoln,
Nebraska: University of Nebraska Press, 1984

Swayne, Zoa L., "Do Them No Harm!" Caldwell, Idaho:
Caxton Press, 2003

## ORDER FORM

Please send me _____ copies of *Native American Women: Three Who Changed History*. I enclose $14.95 for each copy, plus $3.95 for shipping per book.

Name:_____

Address:_____

City/State/Zip: _____

Phone number:_____

My check, payable to Gloria S. Linkey, in the amount of _____ is enclosed.

### MAIL TO:

Gloria S. Linkey
Seacove Publications
561 Bonnie Court
Seaside, Or. 97138

*Orders usually shipped within one business week.*